FLORENCE

Travel Guide and Activity Book for Kids

Elena Gursky

IN THIS BOOK

BEFORE YOU GO

ACTIVITIES

BEFORE YOU GO

ITALIA

TORINO

MILANO

VENEZIA

FIRENZE

ROMA

NAPOLI

PALERMO

DID YOU KNOW?

Florence is called *Firenze* in Italian. Read the next page to find out how Firenze got its name!

CHECK IT OUT!
You can easily pick out Italy on a map because it is shaped like a boot with a heel!

A LITTLE BIT OF HISTORY

Like a lot of cities in Italy, Florence was settled by the ancient Romans.
Firenze comes from Florentiae, a name conveying good luck, from the Latin verb *florēre*, 'to blossom'.

Florence was a center of medieval European trade and finance and one of the wealthiest cities of the Middle Ages. It is also considered to have been the birthplace of the Renaissance. During this time, Florence rose to a position of enormous influence in Italy, Europe, and beyond.

The powerful Medici family paid for the construction of Florence's cathedral and were patrons (financial supporters) of some of the most famous artists and scientists of the Renaissance. Florence's history is very much intertwined with the history of this family.

PARLI ITALIANO?

CIAO!
(**Hi!** say it like "chow")

ARRIVEDERCI!
(**Goodbye!** say it like "arriva-dairchi")

BUONGIORNO!
(**Hello!** say it like "bwohn-jorno")

BUONASERA
(**Good evening!** say it like "bwohna-sara")

3

SCUSI!

(**Excuse me!** Say it like "skoozee")

GRAZIE!

(**Thank you!** Say it like "gratzi-eh")

PER FAVORE!

(**Please!** Say it like "pair favor-eh")

FUN FACTS

PAVING THE WAY

In 1339, Florence became the first city in Europe to pave its streets. Many of its narrow and winding streets today are still paved with cobblestone. Watch your step!

A NEW TUNE

Did you know that the piano was most likely invented in Florence? Bartolomeo Cristofori probably invented the piano while employed by the Medici family. An inventory of instruments shows that a *pianoforte* (piano) was present at court as early as 1700.

FLORENCE AT HOGWARTS

Il porcellino (the little pig) is the nickname for this bronze statue of a boar. You can see the original at Museo Bardini and a copy at the Mercato Nuovo.
But did you know that another copy of the statue is seen briefly in *Harry Potter and the Chamber of Secrets* (2002)? It also appears in *Harry Potter and the Deathly Hallows –Part 2* (2011).

SAY CHEESE!

There are many vintage photo booths from the 1950s still in use throughout the city. It only costs 2€ for 4 pictures! You can find the nearest photo booth at:

www.fotoautomatica.com/fotoautomatica.com/Dove.html

STICK YOUR PHOTOS HERE!

ARCHITECTURE IN FLORENCE

Colorful marble was used to decorate many churches and buildings in Florence. White, pink, and green marble can all be found in nature in Tuscany (the region around Florence). The white marble comes from Carrara and is the most famous and sought-after marble in the world. Famous sculptors like Michelangelo used this marble to make statues.

Can you find these buildings on your trip?

1.

2.

3.

1. Abbazia di San Miniato 2. Baptistry of Santa Maria del Fiore 3. Santa Maria Novella

Use the space on the next page to draw your favorite buildings that you see while in Florence.

MANGIAMO! LET'S EAT!

PLAIN BREAD

Yes, you're reading that right. Florentine bread is famously un-salted, a reminder of a war with neighboring Pisa in which it was difficult to get salt. This bread is not much on its own, but it's a great base for salami, cheese, and spreads.

MY RATING: ☆☆☆☆☆

CROSTINI AI FEGATINI

Speaking of spreads, this one is made with chicken livers, capers, and anchovies.

MY RATING: ☆☆☆☆☆

RIBOLLITA

What about the leftover bread? Florentines use it to make ribollita, a vegetable soup thickened with stale bread.

MY RATING: ☆☆☆☆☆

PAPPARDELLE AL RAGÙ

Pappardelle are long, flat noodles. In Tuscany, they are often served with a ragù (meat sauce) made with game such as *cinghiale* (wild boar) or *lepre* (hare).

MY RATING: ☆☆☆☆☆

BISTECCA ALLA FIORENTINA

Fiorentina means "from Florence". A Fiorentina is a huge steak that is grilled over a fire and oftentimes seasoned with rosemary. Most of the time they are so big that you need to split them with 1 or 2 other people!

MY RATING: ☆☆☆☆☆

GELATO

Gelato (ice cream) is popular everywhere in Italy, but it was born in Florence in the 1500s when Cosimo Ruggeri presented it at the court of Catherine de' Medici, in a competition for the "most unique dish ever seen".

MY RATING: ☆☆☆☆☆

ACTIVITIES

PALAZZO VECCHIO

The Palazzo Vecchio, (pronounced "pa-latzo veck-ee-o") was built in 1299 as the seat of the Signoria, or the ruling body of the Republic of Florence. It was actually called Palazzo della Signoria at this time.

It later served as Duke Cosimo I de' Medici's palace before he decided to move to Palazzo Pitti, giving Palazzo Vecchio its name: Palazzo Vecchio means "old palace" in Italian!

Much, much later, the palace became the seat of united Italy's temporary government from 1865 to 1871.

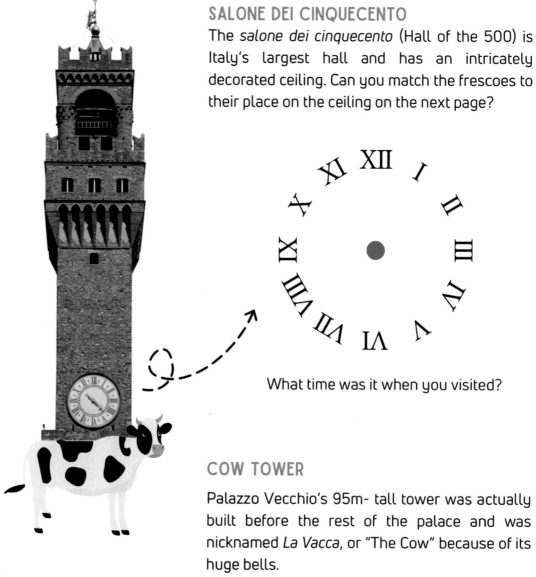

SALONE DEI CINQUECENTO

The *salone dei cinquecento* (Hall of the 500) is Italy's largest hall and has an intricately decorated ceiling. Can you match the frescoes to their place on the ceiling on the next page?

What time was it when you visited?

COW TOWER

Palazzo Vecchio's 95m- tall tower was actually built before the rest of the palace and was nicknamed *La Vacca*, or "The Cow" because of its huge bells.

1.

2.

3.

4.

5.

6.

FIND SOMETHING...

While visiting Palazzo Vecchio's colorful rooms, find an object of each color and then draw a picture of what you found in each circle!

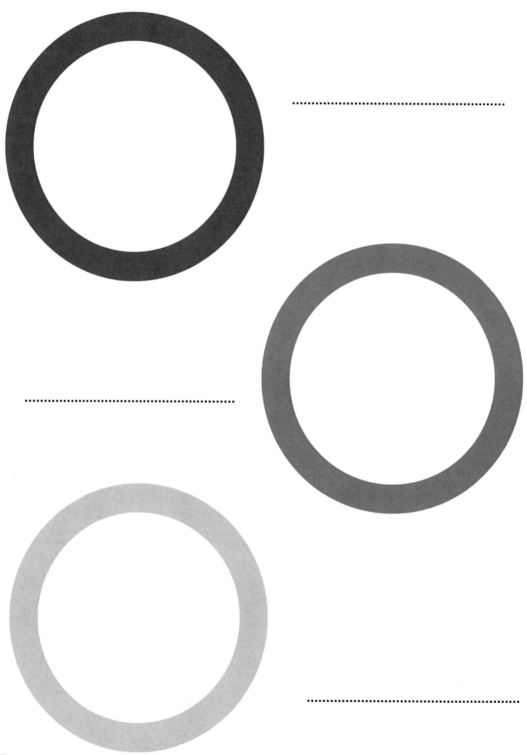

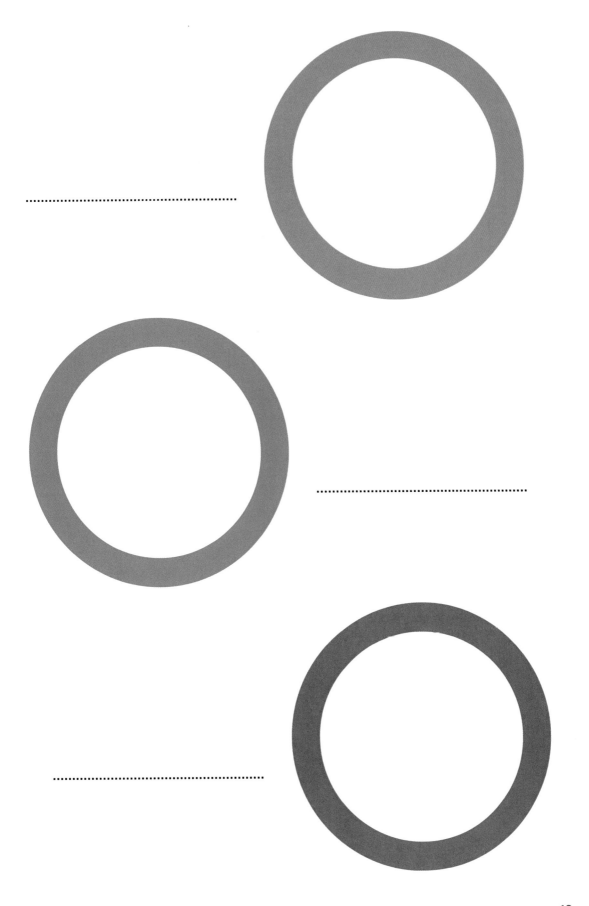

THE UFFIZI

The Uffizi Gallery is one of the most famous art museums in the world. Its collection is huge and it holds some of the world's best-known pieces of Renaissance art.

JUST FOR KIDS

The Uffizi has a Kids section on its website where you can download scavenger hunts and other activities. Visit their site for more information:

www.uffizi.it/en/pages/uffizi-kids

GETTING AROUND

The gallery is 13,000 square meters (139,000 square feet) big. That's the size of about 2.5 professional football fields! It's easy to get lost walking in its 45 halls. Can you solve the maze and reach Caravaggio's painting of Bacchus?

THE BIRTH OF VENUS BY SANDRO BOTTICELLI
Can you finish the picture?

PORTRAITURE

Before there were cameras and smartphones, rich families would pay artists to paint portraits of family members. Can you find these portraits?

☐ PORTRAIT OF FRANCESCO
MARIA DELLA ROVERE
TITIAN

☐ THE DUKE AND DUCHESS OF
URBINO FEDERICO DA
MONTEFELTRO AND BATTISTA
SFORZA

PIERO DELLA FRANCESCA

Your turn! Have a friend or family member face towards the side. Then, draw a portrait of them. Copy the shape of their forehead, nose, lips, and chin.

LOGGIA DEI LANZI

The Loggia dei Lanzi, also called the Loggia della Signoria, is a space on a corner of the Piazza della Signoria and attached to the Uffizi Gallery. It has wide arches open to the street and contains many sculptures. It's basically an open-air sculpture museum!

Prudence

Temperance

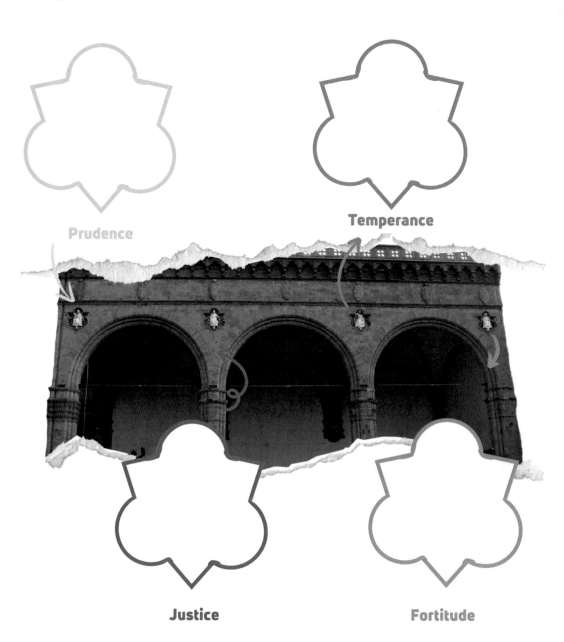

Justice

Fortitude

THE FOUR VIRTUES

Above the arches, there are four statues representing Aristotle's Four Virtues. Aristotle was a philosopher in ancient Greece and described these virtues as the characteristics of a good person.

Prudence: the wisdom to know what is right, even in difficult situations.
Justice: acting fairly towards others
Temperance: only taking what is needed
Fortitude: the courage to do the right thing

Do you know someone with these characteristics? Draw them in place of the statues!

PERSEUS'S HELMET

TAKE A CLOSER LOOK

Look for the statue of Perseus holding the head of Medusa. If you look closely at the back of Perseus's helmet, you'll find a secret self-potrait of the artist, Cellini.

BOBOLI GARDENS

There are lots of statues in the Boboli Gardens (*Giardini di Boboli*). Can you try to recreate them? Take a picture next to each statue! Then, print out the pictures and glue them onto this page.

READY TO BE A STATUE?

NATURE SCAVENGER HUNT

Can you find these things?

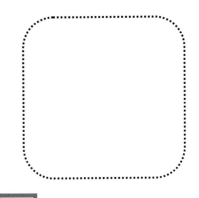

☐ Lily pad

☐ Leaf- draw it!

☐ Pinecone

☐ Turtle

Flower

Duck

What else did you find?

PONTE VECCHIO

Ponte Vecchio means "old bridge" in Italian. But walking over it, you'd forget you were on a bridge! There are shops and houses on each side of the bridge, suspended over the water!

COLOR THE BRIDGE AND THE SHOPS!

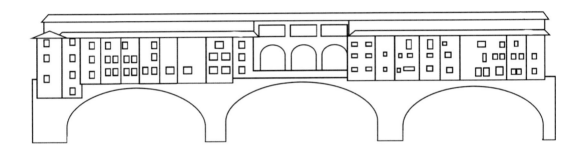

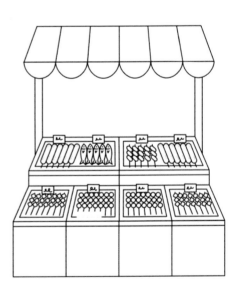

LA BERTA

FOLLOW THE TREASURE MAP TO FIND A SURPRISE!

After you've found the surprise, read about what you found on page 36.

1. STAND IN FRONT OF SANTA MARIA MAGGIORE CHURCH.

2. TURN RIGHT ON VIA DEI CERRETANI, TO THE LEFT OF THE CHURCH.

3. LOOK BETWEEN THE TOP TWO WINDOWS ON THE SIDE OF THE CHURCH.

X MARKS THE SPOT!

DRAW WHAT YOU FIND!

You should see a statue of a face!

SANTA MARIA DEL FIORE

Santa Maria del Fiore, Italian for "Saint Mary of the Flower", is Florence's cathedral (the city's principal church). Construction started on the church in 1296, but after 100 years it was still missing its dome! Many people submitted their designs for the dome, but it was a goldsmith named Filippo Brunelleschi who eventually won the contest to design and finish the dome.

Because of its size, Brunelleschi had to think of special ways to keep the dome from falling down, as well as new machinery to build it. It is still the world's largest masonry (made of brick) dome in the world to this day!

DESIGN YOUR OWN DOME!

29

LEARN MORE ABOUT THE DOME

 Visit this link to watch National Geographic's video about Brunelleschi's dome:

www.youtube.com/watch?v=_IOPIGPQPuM

BUILD A DOME!

Paper models are used by architects to create mini versions of their designs before construction begins. Nowadays, they can also use computers to create 3D models that look and behave exactly like the real-life version.

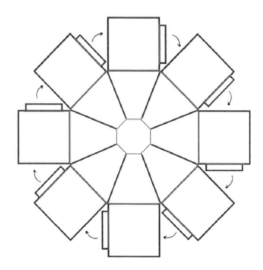

Follow the instructions on the last page of this book to complete your own dome. You'll need:
- scissors
- glue or tape
- colored pencils

AT THE TOP OF THE DOME

Did you know you can climb up 463 steps to reach the top of the dome? There isn't an elevator, but the view is worth it!
Can you find these landmarks in the Florence skyline?

☐ PALAZZO STROZZI

☐ GIOTTO'S BELL TOWER

☐ PIAZZA DELLA REPUBBLICA GALLERY

BADIA FIORENTINA
MONASTERY

PALAZZO VECCHIO

BASILICA DI SAN MINIATO

MARZOCCO

Marzocco the lion is the symbol and protector of Florence. The statue of Marzocco in Piazza della Signoria is a copy of a copy of the original. Did you get that? The original dates back to 1377, but was lost at some point in history. The statue that now stands in Piazza della Signoria is a copy of a statue by Donatello (the real one is in the Bargello museum).

Marzocco was so important to Florentines that prisoners of war from the neighboring town of Pisa were forced to kiss the statue when they were captured!

Marzocco was also was pictured on Tuscany's first postal stamp in 1851!

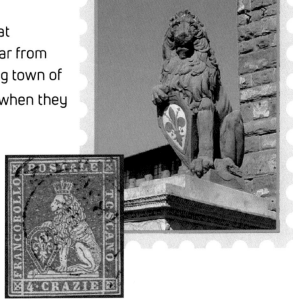

But Marzocco isn't the only lion in Florence! Keep your eyes open for his friends.

COLOR THE LION!

LION BINGO

Can you find these lions? Challenge a friend or family member to lion bingo! Every time you find a lion, put an X through the square. Use the empty squares to draw other lions you find. The first to get 3 lions in a row wins!

My bingo card: ⋯⋯⋯⋯⋯⋯⋯⋯⋯⋯⋯⋯⋯⋯⋯⋯⋯⋯⋯⋯⋯⋯⋯⋯⋯⋯⋯⋯⋯⋯⋯⋯⋯⋯⋯⋯⋯⋯

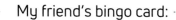
My friend's bingo card: ⋯⋯⋯⋯⋯⋯⋯⋯⋯⋯⋯⋯⋯⋯⋯⋯⋯⋯⋯⋯⋯⋯⋯⋯⋯⋯⋯⋯⋯⋯⋯⋯

My bingo card: ....

Where I found lions:

....

....

....

My friend's bingo card: ....

Where I found lions:

....

....

....

DANTE'S FLORENCE

Dante Alighieri, simply known as Dante, was an Italian poet and philosopher born in Florence in 1625. He was best known for writing *The Divine Comedy,* which is considered the greatest work written in Italian. Dante was famous for writing in Italian at a time when most writers and poets wrote in Latin. This made his work readable for everyone, not just rich people who studied Latin.

DO YOU KNOW ANY LATIN?

Latin	Italian	English
Salve	Buongiorno (but you can also say "Ciao" or even "Salve"!	Hello
Gratias tibi ago	Grazie	Thank you
Vale	Arrivederci	Goodbye
Quid agis	Come stai?	How are you?
Bene/male	Bene/male	Good/bad

DANTE'S ROCK

Legend has it that Dante used to sit on a rock in Piazza delle Pallottole to think and observe the construction of Santa Maria del Fiore.
Can you find it?

DANTE'S HIDDEN PORTRAIT

If you visit Dante's house in via Santa Margherita, take a look at the ground outside. If you look closely, you might be able to spot Dante's profile carved into the stone pavement.

TIP: Some water will help reveal the portrait!

What do you think a Medieval house looks like?
Visit Dante's house to find out!

A DIFFERENT PORTRAIT

Dante's portrait is shown on the back of an Italian coin.
Can you figure out which one?
Draw the other side of the coin!

LEARN MORE ABOUT LA BERTA (FROM PAGE 27)

Did you find Berta's head? How do you think it got there?

The most popular story says the head belongs to a woman who was petrified on September 16, 1326. According to this myth, the woman was a victim of Cecco d'Ascoli, an astrologer who was on his way to prison for heresy (saying things against what the Church believed). As he was brought along Via dei Cerretani, he stopped to ask for some water. Little did he know that looking out a church window was Berta, who at that very moment told the people with him to not allow him a drink. Berta claimed the man was an alchemist who could communicate with the devil using water, and that the devil would set him free if he touched water. Angered, D'Ascoli cast a curse on Berta, preventing her from ever moving.

There is also a more believable story behind the head. One theory says the head is a memorial to the grocery store owner who donated bells to the church. This would explain why it sticks out the bell tower wall and not a window.

What do you think? Write your own story!

....

....

....

....

....

....

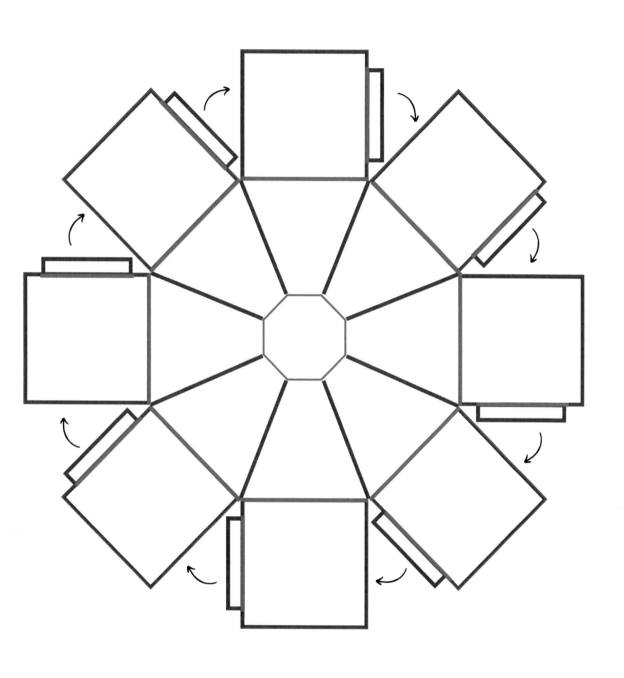

1.COLOR   2. CUT RED LINES   3. FOLD GREEN LINES   4. GLUE TABS

WORKS CITED

Carney, Rob. "Architecture of Florence, Tuscany, Italy." Architecture of Cities, 17 Sept. 2023, architectureofcities.com/florence#elements.

Daniele. "Curiosità Da Vedere a Firenze: Allo Scoperta Di Una Firenze Insolita e Alternativa (Guida 2024)." Gayly Planet, 9 Feb. 2024, www.wearegaylyplanet.com/firenze-insolita-segreta-cosa-vedere/.

Di Ferdinando, Roberto. "Il Profilo Di Dante Sul Lastricato." Curiosita Di Firenze, 15 Dec. 2013, curiositadifirenze.blogspot.com/2013/12/il-profilo-di-dante-sul-lastricato.html.

"Florence." Wikipedia, Wikimedia Foundation, 31 Mar. 2024, en.wikipedia.org/wiki/Florence.

hapichapi. "La Berta." Atlas Obscura, Atlas Obscura, 21 June 2019, www.atlasobscura.com/places/la-berta.

Hunt, Phoebe. "41/2 Minutes: The Story behind Fotoautomatica." The Florentine, 24 Feb. 2022, www.theflorentine.net/2022/02/10/4%C2%BD-minutes-the-story-behind-fotoautomatica/.

"Latin/Common Phrases." Wikiversity, Wikipedia , en.wikiversity.org/wiki/Latin/Common_Phrases. Accessed 7 Apr. 2024.

Macchiavelli, Deborah. "La Storia Del Marzocco, Il Leone Che Protegge Firenze." FirenzeToday, City News, www.firenzetoday.it/cronaca/leone-marzocco-firenze.html. Accessed 7 Apr. 2024.

Maio, Giulia. "Firenze Segreta e Insolita: 10 Cose Curiose Da Vedere a Firenze - Noncieromaistata: Travel Blogger: Giulia Maio." Noncieromaistata, 25 Feb. 2024, www.noncieromaistata.com/2024/02/25/firenze-segreta-e-insolita-10-cose-cuiose-da-vedere-a-firenze/.

"Paintings of the Ceiling of the Hall of Five Hundred of the Palazzo Vecchio in Florence." Visit Florence Italy, 1 Jan. 1970, www.visit-florence-italy.com/museums/palazzo-vecchio/ceiling-paintings-hall-five-hundred-palazzo-vecchio-florence-italy.html.

"Palazzo Vecchio." Wikipedia, Wikimedia Foundation, 23 Mar. 2024, en.wikipedia.org/wiki/Palazzo_Vecchio.

"Porcellino." Wikipedia, Wikimedia Foundation, 27 Mar. 2024, en.wikipedia.org/wiki/Porcellino.

PHOTO CREDITS

Made in the USA
Las Vegas, NV
07 November 2024

11311628R00031